A New Start

Start ONE CHILD'S STRUGGLE WITH OBESITY

ROSANNE SHERITZ SARTORI

A New Start:
One Child's Struggle With Obesity
Grades 2-6

$19.95
ISBN 1-931636-33-8

Written by: Rosanne Sheritz Sartori
Cover Design and Layout by Contract: Ashley S. Linn

Published by: National Center for Youth Issues
                                                                 P.O. Box 22185
                                                                 Chattanooga, Tennessee 37422-2185
                                                                 1-800-477-8277
                                                                 www.ncyi.org

Printed in the United States of America

DEDICATION

This book is dedicated to all the kids who are frustrated and don't know where and how to start. There is hope and you *can* do what you set out to do.

It is also dedicated to my husband, Glenn, who almost always makes wise food and exercise choices.

A New Start published by National Center for Youth Issues, Chattanooga, TN.

ABOUT THE AUTHOR

Rosanne Sheritz Sartori spent 30 years as an educator and retired in 2002. As a classroom teacher and then as an elementary counselor, she worked to help kids conquer any problems they might face. She truly believes that people can achieve the goals they set if they believe they can.

Her previous published resources include **Lively Lessons for Classroom Sessions** and **More Lively Lessons for Classroom Sessions**. She also has written a K-5 **Stand Up Against Bullies** curriculum that will soon be published. She has presented many of her original ideas for stories and lessons at character conferences and counselors' conventions.

She lives with her husband, Glenn, in St. Louis, MO and currently works part-time at a women's fitness center.

TABLE OF CONTENTS

A New Start published by National Center for Youth Issues, Chattanooga, TN.

INTRODUCTION FOR KIDS

Right now there is a big problem in the United States. That problem is obesity. New studies have shown that one in every five kids is overweight and that number is growing.

It's very difficult to eat the right foods, because everywhere you turn there are fast food restaurants and commercials on fast foods, sweet treats and snacks.

It is very difficult to get the right amount of exercise, because there is homework to do and TV to watch and video games to play and besides that, it isn't always safe for a kid to go outside by himself or herself and run around and play.

In "A New Start," a 4th grade boy named Randall Garrett had that problem. He had to learn for himself how to solve it. Maybe what he learned can help you.

It's time for "A New Start!"

A New Start published by National Center for Youth Issues, Chattanooga, TN.

THE STORY...

A New Start

ONE CHILD'S
STRUGGLE
WITH
OBESITY

ROSANNE SHERITZ SARTORI

9

A New Start published by National Center for Youth Issues, Chattanooga, TN.

THE STORY...

CHAPTER 1—THE WORST DAY EVER

Randall Garrett was a 9-year-old boy who enjoyed school, watching TV, playing video games and being with his friends. He was an only child and he lived with his mom in a small house, not too far from school.

If you asked someone who knew Randall to describe him, that person might say that he was smart, kind and friendly. One more descriptive adjective that person might use for Randall was "big."

Yes, Randall Garrett could certainly be considered "big." In fact, his whole family, which included his grandma and grandpa, two aunts and one uncle, was "big." At least that is what Randall's mother called it. The kids at school called it "fat."

According to his mother's stories, Randall had been born big. Randall's mom had always stated with motherly pride that he was the biggest baby in the maternity room at the hospital, and that fact didn't change with age.

Randall could never remember a time that he wasn't bigger than all the other kids his age. He had always worn clothes that were labeled "husky," and his mom had always told him that he had a little "baby fat" on him that would disappear as he got older.

When he was in Kindergarten and 1st grade, Randall didn't mind being big at all. Nobody cared much about his size because Randall was nice and he was fun to play with. He played with the kids and enjoyed school. The only activity he couldn't take a part in was the seesaw. He couldn't seesaw with any other kid, because the seesaw would stay down on his side when he sat on it. But other than being excluded from this one activity, Randall was happy and had fun with his friends.

11

As he got older, his size increased and some of the kids at school started making mean comments about his weight. There were kids, like Mike, Dominic and Keisha, who made fun of him and called him a "fat pig." Randall always felt very bad when that happened, but he tried his best to ignore these comments and to stay close to his friends, Patrick and Jamal, who accepted him as he was.

His size began bothering him more as he got into second and then in third grade because of the rude comments he began hearing more often. He tried not to do anything that would call attention to his size. So every year he really hated the gym class when the gym teacher would weigh and measure all of the kids. The teacher would put these numbers on a chart for the whole class to see. Naturally, there were always a few comments from the rest of the kids in class about how much Randall weighed.

As he reached the end of third grade, Randall's weight began to bother him even more. It wasn't just because of what the other kids thought and said about him, but now even when he was alone, Randall was beginning to feel discouraged by his bulk. It was getting harder for him to move around and play games. The only times he completely forgot about his size was when he was playing video games with his friends, while he was watching TV and when he was at home talking with his mom, who loved him, no matter what.

13

A New Start published by National Center for Youth Issues, Chattanooga, TN.

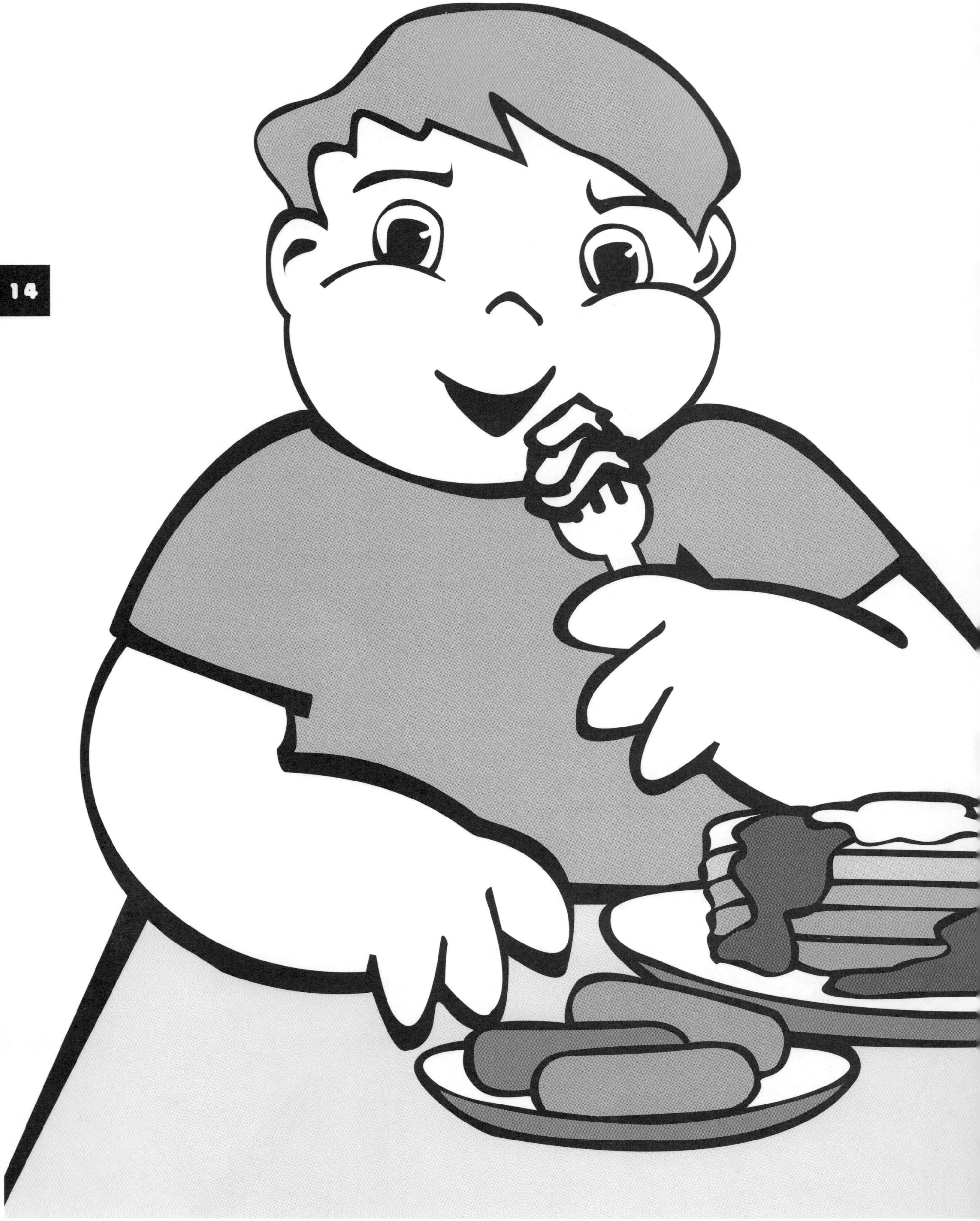

The very first day of fourth grade turned out to be the worst day of Randall's life. The most embarrassing thing that could ever happen to a kid took place on a day that should have been a happy one.

The morning had started out bright and cheerful. Randall did well in school and had been very excited to begin a fresh new school year. He was thrilled when he found out that he had Mrs. Henderson as a teacher, because everyone knew she was the nicest fourth grade teacher at Jefferson Elementary; and to top it off … his best friend, Jamal, was going to be in his class! What more could a boy want?

He had brand new school supplies, loaded into a brand new book bag. His mom had cooked his favorite breakfast—pancakes and sausages— and he was off to what should have been a perfect day to start a new school year.

Everything was fine until he arrived at school. As the kids filed in, they hung up their jackets on a hook and were told to find a desk. On that first day, Mrs. Henderson was going to let them sit anywhere they wanted. Jamal motioned Randall over to a desk near the windows. And that is when the horrible thing happened.

15

A New Start published by National Center for Youth Issues, Chattanooga, TN.

As Randall went to sit down at the desk, he realized that he couldn't fit in the chair. He tried squeezing himself, sucking in his breath, but he could not get his body into the space between the chair and the desk. He didn't know what to do. He just stood there. Meanwhile, Mrs. Henderson had asked everyone to sit down. But Randall just stood there. Mrs. Henderson looked up at him and asked him if he had a problem.

Randall said very quietly, "I can't fit in my desk."

The kids nearby had been staring at him and heard what he said, but Mrs. Henderson was busy with taking roll and checking the class list and didn't hear him. She looked up again, saw him still standing there and asked again why he wasn't seated.

With his face bright red and feeling as if he could cry at any moment, Randall had to say it louder. "I'm sorry, Mrs. Henderson, I can't sit down because I can't fit in the seat."

Several of the children snickered, and Mike elbowed Dominic, but since it was the first day of school and the kids wanted to make a good impression on their new teacher, they didn't make any cracks or laugh out loud. Still Randall felt so embarrassed that he wanted to disappear right then. He wished he could be anywhere else in the world instead of in Mrs. Henderson's fourth grade classroom.

The teacher never meant to embarrass Randall. There was sympathy on her face as she quickly went over to him and gently took his arm. "Here, Randall," she said, "sit here."

Mrs. Henderson led him to the back table and told him that he could sit on her chair until she got one that would fit him. Randall was so humiliated that he felt sick to his stomach. He did not want to sit on the teacher's chair and he did not want to sit at the back table. He wanted to sit in a desk like every other kid in his class.

Randall spent the most miserable day of his life on that first day of fourth grade. He didn't even hear what his new teacher had to say about the class rules and classroom management procedures. He wanted the day to be over quickly, but it seemed to drag on forever.

A New Start published by National Center for Youth Issues, Chattanooga, TN.

A New Start published by National Center for Youth Issues, Chattanooga, TN.

CHAPTER 2—CHANGES ARE COMING

As soon as he got home, Randall wanted to forget about everything that had happened. The first thing he did was go straight to the cookie jar. Cookies were his favorite snack and always made him feel better, when things weren't going his way. He opened the jar and was happy to see that his mom had baked a fresh batch of chocolate chip cookies to celebrate his first day of fourth grade. Randall grabbed a handful of cookies, poured himself some orange drink and walked over to turn on the TV. His favorite programs were on right after school and he wanted something … anything to take his mind off of the terrible day he had experienced. He watched the TV as he munched on the cookies. But as hard as he tried, he could not take his mind off of the day he had just endured.

He pictured in his mind how his teacher had stood by her desk, until the janitor had brought in a new teacher's chair for her at mid-morning. Randall had tried to act as if everything was okay, but it wasn't okay. He had tried not to make eye contact with anyone. All he had thought about was that he never wanted to come back to this class and never wanted to sit at this table again.

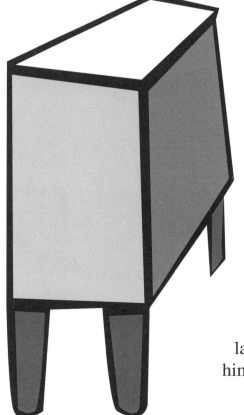

While continuing to munch and watch TV, Randall's thoughts drifted back to lunch and recess, when his friends, Jamal and Patrick, had tried very hard not to mention Randall's "desk assignment" though it was obviously on everyone's mind. He also remembered seeing several kids pointing, laughing and whispering about him and his seating problem.

A New Start published by National Center for Youth Issues, Chattanooga, TN.

As he was rewinding the terrible day over and over again in his mind, Randall's mother came home from the errand she had been running. She smiled and asked, "How was your first day of fourth grade?"

Then before waiting for an answer, she said, "Fourth grade… I can't believe how big you are getting!" She said these words very innocently, not knowing how they were being received.

Randall muttered that his day had been okay. He was too humiliated to tell her what had happened. But his mom was pretty good at reading his moods and she pressed him for more details of the day.

She asked, "Is something wrong? Wasn't your teacher nice? Did you have a disagreement with Patrick or Jamal?"

Randall said abruptly, "Mom, everything was fine. Now leave me alone!"

His mother looked hurt for a moment, but then said, "Well, at least we will have a good meal for supper. I made one of your favorites—macaroni and cheese, to celebrate the first day of school."

Randall brightened at that bit of news. He loved macaroni and cheese!

"Thanks Mom," he said, "school was really okay. I guess it is just different being in fourth grade."

During dinner he told her about his day. He told her that his teacher seemed nice, that all the subjects seemed familiar, and that Jamal was in his class. He told her everything… except for the fact that he was sitting at a table instead of a desk.

After dinner, as his mom cleaned up the kitchen, Randall played his favorite video games and then at 9:00, he got ready for bed.

Somehow, he had to face the next day at school. He dreaded sitting at that back table, but he resigned himself that it would be okay.

21

A New Start published by National Center for Youth Issues, Chattanooga, TN.

A New Start published by National Center for Youth Issues, Chattanooga, TN.

On the second day of school, during silent reading time, he looked up from his book and looked around the room, staring at the backs of the other kids. He noticed that he wasn't the only "big" kid in the room. Maria, Latisha and Clark were pretty big. So were Juan and Kendall. But they all fit in their desks and this proved to Randall that he was certainly the biggest kid in his class.

At recess, while sitting on a bench at the side of the playground, Randall continued his study of the kids in his classroom. The skinny kids seemed to have so much energy! They ran, played kickball, hopscotch and tag. Randall noticed that some of the "bigger" kids were playing games too, but they were games that didn't involve a lot of movement.

Somehow, Randall got through that second day of school, much as he did the first. He was starting to get used to his position at the back table and not too many people said anything about where he was sitting. Of course, Mike and Dominic made some rude remarks about it, and he was pretty sure some of the girls had been laughing about it, but again Randall tried hard not to pay attention.

What Randall didn't know was that the third day of fourth grade was going to be a day that would change his life forever. It started out as a normal day. His mom made waffles with blueberry syrup for breakfast and he washed it down with a glass of grape juice.

After his meal, he got his things together, put on his jacket and waited at the bus stop with the usual group of neighborhood kids.

23

He had just settled into his chair at the back of the classroom when Mrs. Henderson announced that the school was going to have a very special assembly that morning. She told the class that the neighboring school, Harrison Elementary School, had a jump rope club and the club members were coming to Jefferson to do a performance. Mrs. Henderson's class walked down to the gym with the rest of the classes, not knowing that they all were in for a real treat.

The assembly started with the gym teacher from Harrison explaining how the jump rope club had started when some of the students got interested in jumping rope. The kids had expressed a desire to start an after-school club and had developed some routines.

The teacher then went on to announce very dramatically, "Without any further introductions, here are the Harrison Hoppers!"

Some loud rock and roll music began to play and kids came out with jump ropes and started jumping to the beat. Did those kids jump rope! The Jefferson kids sitting in the audience were completely mesmerized with the intricate routines the Harrison Hoppers performed. They jumped individually to the beat, moved in and out of other kids' jump ropes; they jumped two together, three together and even five together, all to the beat of the music. The "Hoppers" did Double Dutch, they criss-crossed ropes, and they performed other fancy tricks that looked impossible to the untrained eye. The assembly turned out to be the liveliest, most entertaining show that Randall had ever seen. He felt a thrill going through his body and from the reaction of his friends, they all felt the same way.

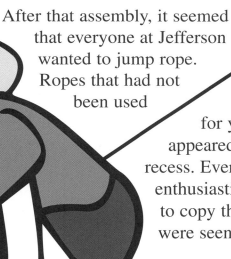

After that assembly, it seemed that everyone at Jefferson wanted to jump rope. Ropes that had not been used for years appeared at the next recess. Everyone was enthusiastically trying to copy the routines that were seen in the assembly.

25

A New Start published by National Center for Youth Issues, Chattanooga, TN.

Randall didn't try jumping that day at recess, because he didn't want to do anything like that in front of other kids. He knew that he was not very light on his feet. But as soon as he got home, he asked his mom if there was any rope around. She found some old rope, on which she had hung wet clothes when the dryer had broken two years ago.

Randall went outside and tried to jump. He couldn't do it. Not only could he not perform the tricks with rope that he had seen, he couldn't jump at all, not even one jump. He was just too big to jump.

He gave up after several attempts and went inside. Happy to see that his mom had refilled the cookie jar, he took a handful and sat down to watch TV. But he couldn't get the assembly out of his mind. It was so cool!

As Randall flipped through the channels, he heard an announcer on TV saying something about childhood obesity. He stopped channel surfing and listened. He heard the reporter say that obesity was a big problem in the United States and that childhood obesity was reaching an all-time high. The reporter went on to say that kids ate too much junk food and didn't get enough exercise.

Randall started to change the channel, but then thought about his own situation. He had never used the word "obese" to describe himself. He didn't even like the word "fat." His mother said he was big, but he didn't fit in his desk and he couldn't jump a rope. Maybe he was obese. He decided to listen to the rest of the report.

The reporter said things that Randall didn't want to hear. She said that kids were eating way too much of the wrong types of foods and they weren't getting enough physical exercise. She said that obese kids often grow up to be obese adults with many different types of medical problems, such as heart trouble, high blood pressure and diabetes. The reporter added that kids didn't even have to wait to be adults to have these problems. There were many kids who were already sick from problems associated with being fat.

A New Start published by National Center for Youth Issues, Chattanooga, TN.

All of a sudden, the happenings of the last three days came whirling through Randall's head … the humiliation of not fitting into a desk, the jump-rope club's show at his school, the news show… it all came together. He didn't want to be obese, he didn't want to be fat … he didn't want to be "big."

Randall said out loud, "I AM GOING TO CHANGE MY LIFE!"

He didn't know what he was going to do, but he knew he didn't want to spend the rest of his life, trapped in this huge body. He had to make some big changes and he had to start today. Randall decided right then that he was going to get a new start in life.

Randall knew he couldn't do this alone. He went into the kitchen to talk to his mom, who was cooking their dinner. She turned toward him when Randall said, "Mom, I am obese and I want to be smaller." His mom looked at him with a shocked expression on her face.

"Randall, you are not obese. You are just big-boned!"

"No Mom, I am obese." He went on to tell her that he didn't fit in a fourth grade desk and that he couldn't jump even one jump with the rope. He told her that he didn't want to live his life this way and he didn't want to get sick. He just wanted to be smaller!

That day in the kitchen Randall and his mom cried together.

When they were finished, Randall said, "Mom, you have to help me because you are the one who cooks the food in our family. I don't know what I am supposed to eat and I can't do this without you."

Randall's mother felt a wave of sympathy for her son. She knew exactly how he felt because she had grown up with the same problem. She knew how it felt to be the biggest kid in the class. She had wanted better for Randall, but he had turned out to be just like her. She loved her son very much and wanted to see him be happy again.

His mom said, "I promise you that I will help you on this new start to be healthy and fit. We will work as partners and tackle this problem together."

Randall smiled and felt better already. With his mom's help he could make this new start come true.

A New Start published by National Center for Youth Issues, Chattanooga, TN.

CHAPTER 3—GATHERING FACTS

Later that evening, Randall and his mom went to the library to do research on how to fight the problem of obesity. They went to the section called, "Health and Fitness," and both began taking books off the shelf that had anything to do with childhood obesity. They were amazed at the amount of information that was in these books. There was so much material that they both felt overwhelmed.

Randall's mom suggested that they start their new project by studying the information published by the United States Department of Agriculture (USDA) and the United States Department of Health and Human Services (DHHS). His mom told Randall that government recommendations would be a safe source of information, since everything had been well-researched and these government agencies seemed to have a lot of material on dietary guidelines and exercise. She told Randall that by sticking to one credible source, they wouldn't get contradictory messages, which would make everything more confusing.

Randall's mom then said, "For the latest, most up-to-date information, we should use a computer instead of using these books that might be out-of-date. Let's use the library computers and search the Internet!"

They found two computers side-by side that weren't being used. They sat down and started looking for advice, by typing "USDA guidelines for childhood obesity" on the search engine that was on the computer screen. Immediately, page after page of links to articles on obesity appeared on the screen. It seemed that there was a lot of advice that could be very helpful in starting their new project. Randall's mom reminded him to limit his search to the articles published by the USDA and DHHS.

A New Start published by National Center for Youth Issues, Chattanooga, TN.

The first thing they both learned was that obesity is a huge problem for adults and kids in the United States. Randall read that currently, one in every five kids is overweight and the number is continuing to grow. Thinking about his classmates, Randall realized that this fact was probably true. It didn't make him feel any better to know that he had a lot of company with the same problem.

After reading a little more, Randall realized that much of what he and his mom had been eating was contributing to their size. Randall learned that the foods he loved to eat, especially when he was having a bad day, were referred to as "comfort foods." Foods like cookies, bread, macaroni, potato chips, pancakes, and waffles might be okay for an occasional treat, but they were not the kind of foods a person needed to be healthy. They had too many calories and not enough vitamins and minerals.

A New Start published by National Center for Youth Issues, Chattanooga, TN.

34

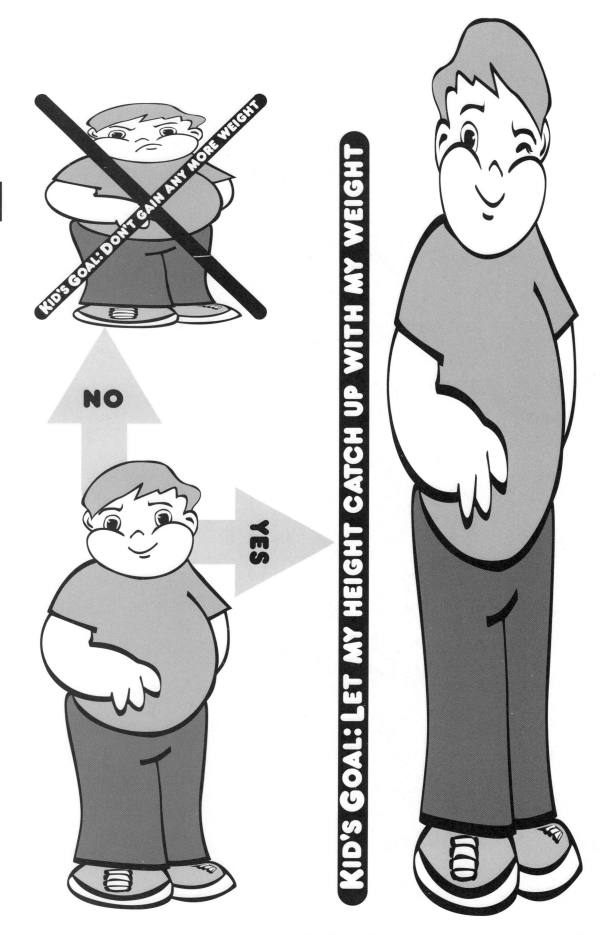

NO

YES

KID'S GOAL: DON'T GAIN ANY MORE WEIGHT

KID'S GOAL: LET MY HEIGHT CATCH UP WITH MY WEIGHT

A New Start published by National Center for Youth Issues, Chattanooga, TN.

A really important fact that his mom learned on that first night of research was that a child Randall's age should probably NOT go on a diet. She told Randall that starting a diet at his age would just trigger unhealthy eating practices. She read aloud from her computer screen and said that what obese kids need to do is to set a goal to become healthy. To do that they would have to learn to eat the right amount of nutritious, healthy foods.

His mom read out loud to Randall, "Obese kids should not try to lose weight, but their goal should be not to gain any more weight. That way, when they grow taller, their height will catch up with their weight."

Next, Randall read information about calories and their relationship to weight. He learned that all food has calories, which is used as fuel by people. Foods that are high in sugar and in fat have a high calorie level. If the calories are not all used up, they will turn into fat. Because Randall was overweight, he realized that he had probably been taking in more calories than he was using up. He thought about the amount of sugar he had been eating and all the hours he had spent watching TV and playing video games. The combination of the two was making him fatter with every passing day!

Randall read further and learned that if a person wants to lose weight, he needs to take in fewer calories than he uses up as energy. Or he could get more exercise so that his body will use the calories he is consuming.

35

After reading a little more, Randall decided that his goal should be to become healthy, not just to lose weight. Eating healthy foods low in sugar and fat and getting more exercise would be best for him! He read an article that said that he should not skip meals or go on any kind of fad diet, because these were practices that were sure to fail and were not healthy. Randall thought to himself, "I'm going to eat the proper amount of healthy foods, which is what I should have been doing all along." He was going to make some needed changes in his eating and exercise habits and it was going to be a permanent life change!

The next screen Randall and his mom both studied was the Food Pyramid, the dietary guideline, published by the USDA. As they studied the Pyramid carefully, they both realized that to be healthy, a person needs to eat a variety of fruits, vegetables, low-fat dairy items, lean meats and whole grain products. His mom promised Randall that she would go grocery shopping while he was at school the next day.

His mom also told him that while he was at school, she was going to clean out the pantry and refrigerator and throw away all the junk food they had in their house. She said that she had just read that junk food, like chips, candy bars and sugary cereals and juices, were filled with empty calories … high in calorie count, but with little nutritional value.

Another thing Randall and his mom realized from studying the Food Pyramid was that they had been eating more than one serving at a time. One slice of bread was considered one serving. A whole sandwich then would be two servings from the bread and grains group. When Randall and his mom ate spaghetti, they probably had been heaping four or five servings on their plate! In fact, Randall thought that he had probably been eating about 25 servings from the Grain Group each day! In order to be healthy, he needed to eat more from other food groups, especially from the Fruits and Vegetables Groups.

Another new thing Randall and his mother learned about serving size was that the way foods are packaged fool many people. Randall and his mom, like many other people, thought that a whole package of potato chips was one serving. But Randall read some information in the USDA guidelines that said that people must read the label on every package carefully, because the label might indicate that there are two or three servings in one package.

37

Randall and his mom both came home from the library excited with the information that they had learned. As they walked in the door, Randall turned on the TV out of habit, and the first thing he saw was a TV commercial, advertising huge hamburgers and gigantic orders of french fries. He had just learned that these foods were not the type of foods that would make him healthy because they were filled with empty calories.

All of a sudden Randall realized how many of these commercials there were on TV. He could practically recite a dozen of them without much effort. He knew that these advertisements were filled with recommendations to buy products, whether they were healthy or not. Right then, he decided that he was going to have to think for himself and not be open to the suggestions of the commercials.

Randall decided that it would be a good idea to watch a lot less TV. He realized that it would probably be a good decision for several reasons. First of all, he wouldn't be tempted by all the commercials. But a second reason was because of something he had just learned at the library—the USDA and DHHS recommends that children should get about 60 minutes of exercise each day—so Randall was not going to have much time for TV. He had also learned a third reason for watching less TV: that many people who eat in front of the TV don't even realize how much they are eating and they end up eating a lot more than they planned. He knew that, in the past, he had eaten whole packages of cookies without even realizing that they were gone, all while watching TV. So along with cutting down on his TV watching, Randall also decided never to eat in front of the TV again!

A New Start published by National Center for Youth Issues, Chattanooga, TN.

NEW START
CONTRACT

CHAPTER 4—STICKING TO IT

The next day after school, Randall went to the doctor. His mother had made the appointment first thing that morning. She told her son that she wanted Dr. Burns to check him out before they started their new eating and exercise plan.

Dr. Burns listened to Randall's heart, took his blood pressure and told him that it would be a wonderful boost to his health to begin eating the proper-sized portions of healthy foods, along with exercise. He gave his seal of approval on the new program that Randall and his mom were about to begin.

Randall knew that to begin this new way of living, he would need a plan. He couldn't wait to get home, so he could start working on it. He asked his mom for help and they sat down together at the kitchen table to work on the plan, the moment they came in from the doctor's office.

As he pulled his chair to the table, he realized that changing his old ways was not going to be easy. He had formed habits that were as old as he was and they would be tough to break. But Randall really wanted a new beginning, more than he wanted his old comfort foods. So he decided to give his new health program a name. He thought of the name "A New Start," because that was exactly what it was.

His mom suggested that they begin with a promise to commit to this new program and stick to it faithfully. She said that they needed a contract. His mom took out a piece of paper and wrote "New Start Contract" at the top. Randall's mom then wrote out her part of the contract: She would supply healthy foods for both of them and would try be a good role model when it came to eating and exercising. She stated in the contract that she would try to motivate Randall when he needed it and that she would be his "New Start" coach.

Randall's part of the contract stated that he would set realistic goals and would work hard to make them come true. He was ready to make a firm commitment to the necessary changes in what he ate and how much he exercised. They both signed and dated the contract. This was an exciting beginning to Randall's "New Start!"

A New Start published by National Center for Youth Issues, Chattanooga, TN.

Then Randall got out another piece of paper and wrote "My Food Goals" at the top. On this paper, Randall decided he would use the USDA's Food Pyramid as an eating guide and make a list of healthy, nutritious foods and the servings he should be eating daily. He knew he was going to miss a lot of his old favorite foods and he didn't care for vegetables very much, but as he pictured himself sitting at the back table in his classroom, he told himself that he was going to have to learn to like vegetables! He decided that he was even going to ask his mom to buy vegetables that he had never wanted to taste before, like asparagus and brussel sprouts!

MY FOOD GOALS

+ Water

Randall knew that he would want a treat now and then, because his new eating plan was not supposed to be a diet, but a new way of eating for the rest of his life. So he wrote down that he would allow himself one "junk food treat" each week and no more. Randall thought that if he planned ahead for the treat, then he would not be as tempted to cheat and go wild!

Another word that he wrote in big letters on the "Food Goals" sheet was "WATER." Randall knew that he was going to have to give up soda, and all the sweet fruit juices he had loved so much. Randall had learned that soda and sugary juices had lots of empty calories. He also didn't want to start drinking diet sodas because they were not as healthy as plain old water.

He sighed as he got up to fill a big glass with nice cold water. This wasn't going to be easy!

43

A New Start published by National Center for Youth Issues, Chattanooga, TN.

MY EXERCISE GOALS

1 HOUR OF EXERCISE EACH DAY

recess

am

dance

A New Start published by National Center for Youth Issues, Chattanooga, TN.

Randall sipped water while he and his mom planned the first week's worth of meals and snacks on a sheet they called "The Weekly Menu." They wrote down the proper amounts of foods using the Food Guide Pyramid. As part of the planning process, they tried to include a variety of all kinds of fruits and vegetables, since Randall had learned that different-colored fruits and vegetables have different vitamins and minerals. To be really healthy, a person needed all kinds of nutrients.

When he and his mom were finished with the menu, Randall got out another piece of paper, which he entitled "My Exercise Goals." He began to think about his exercise plan. He really wanted to jump rope, but he knew he wasn't capable of that just yet. Being realistic, Randall thought he had better start his exercise program by doing something he could do … walk! Randall knew that since he was so heavy, he might have to take it slowly for a while. But since the doctor had given the okay, he was going to pick up the pace as soon as he could so that he could get his heart pumping hard and burn some calories!

He wrote on the sheet that he would take a 30-minute walk every day and then in addition to walking at recess. He also decided to burn extra energy any time he could, like taking the stairs instead of elevators and asking his mom to park farther out in the parking lots of the stores where they shopped.

While thinking of other ways to get some exercise so that it would add up to an hour a day, Randall thought that he might try dancing to the music he loved hearing on the radio. He pictured himself and thought that he would probably look very silly doing this activity, but he would do it privately in his room and at least he would be moving! Every bit of exercise he did would help him achieve his "New Start." He figured out that walking in the morning, and at recess, and dancing in his room would add up to one hour of exercise each day.

45

Since Randall knew it wasn't safe for a kid to go out walking alone, he asked his mom if she would walk with him in the morning. She reminded him that she was his partner and that she would love to walk with him. She told him that they would encourage each other and the exercise would certainly be good for her too.

They began the "New Start" plan the very next day. Randall's mom woke him up an hour before his usual time and said it was time for their walk. He started to complain and roll over, but then he remembered how much he hated sitting at that back table in school. All of his new goals came flooding back to his mind. He quickly got up, got dressed and went for a walk with his mom.

They decided on that first walk to start each day just like this. No matter what the weather was like, they were going to walk. If it was cold, they would put on layers of clothes; if it rained, they would carry umbrellas. They both decided to allow no excuses from each other – they would walk each and every morning!

After a week of sticking to this agreement, they both realized that the daily walk really wasn't bad. It quickly became a habit to wake up early and go out on their walk before breakfast. Randall and his mom began to see the same people each morning … the newspaper delivery guy, the neighbor who left for work exactly at 6:00 every morning, and the high school kids waiting for their school bus. Randall and his mom would wave and smile, and they really began to look forward to seeing these special people each day.

While on these walks, Randall and his mom always talked and planned what they would eat that day. Breakfast no longer consisted of pancakes or waffles with syrup. Now they were eating oatmeal without extra sugar added, fruit and low-fat milk.

Randall and his mom were both eating so much healthier than they used to eat. His mom had learned all kinds of new recipes that made vegetables taste great and even Randall had learned to cook and occasionally take his turn in the kitchen.

They continued to do research on how to fight obesity. Randall and his mom learned that it was helpful to eat small bites of food slowly. Before their "New Start" they used to eat so fast that they didn't even realize when they were full. They also learned that it was not a good idea to eat before bedtime, because those calories were not going to be burned while they were sleeping! Randall set a rule that he would eat his last meal three hours before bedtime.

47

A New Start published by National Center for Youth Issues, Chattanooga, TN.

48

A New Start published by National Center for Youth Issues, Chattanooga, TN.

Another new habit Randall and his mom learned was to study labels on foods at the grocery store, checking for the ingredients. Randall never realized that there were so many names for sugar! Some of his old favorite foods had ingredients like dextrose, fructose, corn syrup, sucrose and malt syrup. Since he was trying to limit his sugar intake, he had to be very careful he wasn't eating lots of sugar under a different name!

Randall's mom refused to buy junk food like chips, corn curls and candy bars anymore. But since she knew that she and her son weren't going to be able to go the rest of their lives without any sweets or snacks, they both went back to the library. They wanted to find out some healthy alternatives to the junky treats they had both loved. There they learned that plain popcorn or a few nuts were better than greasy potato chips and they learned that cookies made from whole wheat and sweetened with honey were better than those from white flour and white sugar. Also, they both learned that it was okay to eat a small treat now and then, just as long as it wasn't an everyday occurrence. Their "New Start" eating program was a healthy food plan, not a diet that would deprive them of every food they had ever enjoyed.

There were some days that Randall really yearned for some of the junk foods he had eaten all his life. Sometimes he missed those old "comfort foods" and felt tempted by the thought of high-fat and sugary foods. But every time he felt that tremendous urge, he would try to remember his goals and the reason he was doing all of this. He pictured the day he had to say to Mrs. Henderson, "I can't fit in my desk." That helped him be strong against the temptation of foods loaded with empty calories. Instead, he would eat a piece of fruit or some raw vegetables his mom kept in the refrigerator for snacks.

A funny thing happened after weeks of avoiding junky foods. Randall's taste buds gradually began to change. Healthy foods started tasting better to him than food loaded with sugar and fat.

One day, he was at Jamal's house and was offered a "regular" chocolate chip cookie. Randall ate the cookie to be polite and found that it didn't even taste that great to him anymore. He liked his mom's homemade whole-wheat nut cookies better. After that incident, Randall learned how to politely refuse offers of sweets and unhealthy food, no matter who offered it.

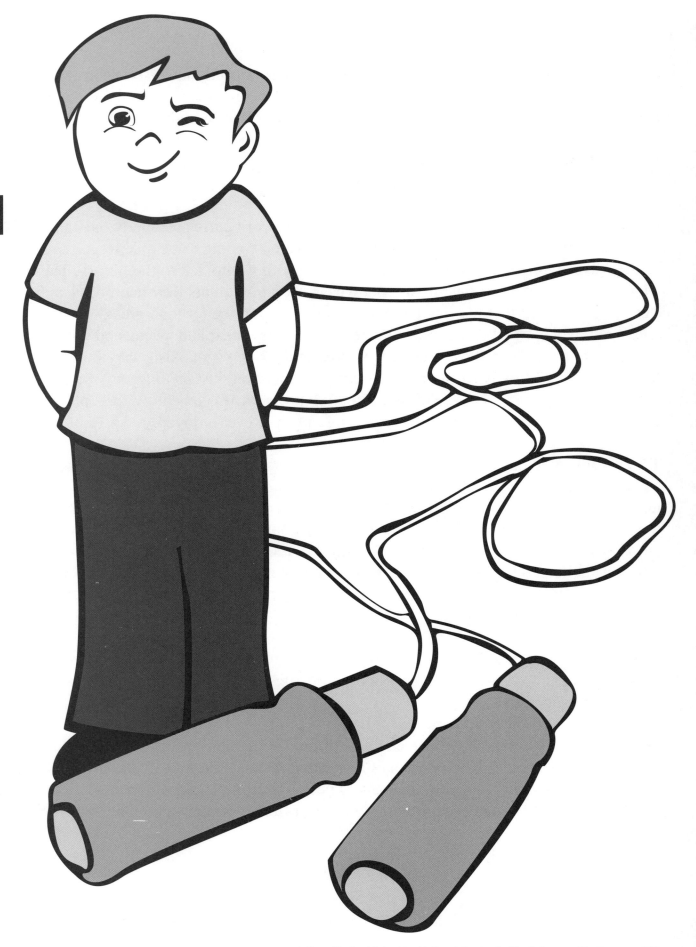

A couple of months after beginning the "New Start," Randall could feel a big difference. He didn't know if he looked any smaller, but he felt better. He had more energy. Now after school, he didn't drop, exhaustedly, in front of the TV. He played outside with Patrick and Jamal and he had even gotten his old bike out of the garage. Randall found that he liked being active, and he started adding more exercise to his schedule… fun games with his friends.

Of course, he still enjoyed going on his daily walk with his mom because they laughed and talked and saw all their morning friends… and after all, it was part of the agreement. Randall kept up with all of his original exercise goals for at least an hour a day and on many days it turned out to be more. At recess, he didn't usually just walk around, he ran and played kickball and soccer with the other kids. Even his dancing skills were improving … although he still didn't want an audience!

One day, Randall saw the rope lying in the garage where he had left it the day of the Harrison Hoppers assembly. He started to wonder, and before long he picked up the rope and jumped. He cleared the rope with no problem. Randall thought to himself, "Wow, maybe I'll put on some music and jump to the music. Maybe I'll organize a jump rope club at school! Maybe we will go perform in other schools!"

As he headed to Patrick's house to tell him about his plan, Randall felt happy. He felt that he had gained power over his life. The dream for the jump rope club could actually happen. Randall knew that he was quite capable of making a plan, setting goals and making them come true. Anything was possible with a "New Start!"

"Hmmm … how does the Jefferson Jumpers sound?" he wondered as he ran all the way to Patrick's house.

51

CHAPTER 5—EPILOGUE

The first day of 5th grade started out as any other day. Randall and his mother took their morning walk, which had expanded from the original half hour walk to a full hour. Since this was the first day of the school year, they saw the high school kids standing on the corner waiting for the bus. The kids called out and waved to Randall and his mom, who waved back.

After the walk, Randall's mom began to prepare breakfast while he got ready for school. He got out his new book bag filled with new school supplies and got dressed in the brand new clothes bought especially for this first day of school.

When he was ready, Randall sat down at the table with his mom to eat breakfast, which consisted of a cup of blueberries, a poached egg served over a piece of whole-wheat toast with some low-fat cheese sauce and a glass of low-fat milk.

Randall's mom wished him luck with his new school year and gave him a kiss. Then he picked up the lunch his mom had packed for him and went out to meet Jamal at the bus stop. This year, Jamal wasn't going to be in his class, but that wasn't going to stop their friendship from continuing.

On the bus, both boys talked excitedly about school and the prospects of being in a brand new grade. They good-naturedly teased each other about who had the best teacher. Randall was sure that his new teacher, Mr. Towers, was the best fifth grade teacher. Jamal said his teacher, Mrs. Davidson, was the best. The boys continued to talk about their teachers, the kids in their classes, and the jump rope club that was going to be meeting today after school. The ride to school seemed short since they had so much to say to each other.

When they arrived at school, they hurriedly made plans to meet at recess, and then headed to their own classrooms. Randall was happy to see his friend Patrick, who was already in the class-room. Patrick motioned for Randall to take the desk next to him. Memories of the first day of fourth grade flitted through Randall's mind, but he knew that this school year was going to have a very different beginning.

As he slid into the desk chair, he looked toward the front of the room and smiled at his new teacher. He was ready for another brand "new start!"

A New Start published by National Center for Youth Issues, Chattanooga, TN.

THE WORKSHEETS

53

A New Start published by National Center for Youth Issues, Chattanooga, TN.

A New Start published by National Center for Youth Issues, Chattanooga, TN.

PICTURE ME

Goal-setting is an important aspect of "A New Start." When setting a goal, it is important to visualize the outcome in your mind and remind yourself of this, every time you feel tempted to stray from the healthy habits you are trying to form.

At the top of the page, draw a picture of what you look like now. On the bottom half of the page, draw a picture of what you will look like and what you will be doing when you have reached your goal. Keep that new picture in your mind as you work toward your goal!

This is a picture of me now.

This is a picture of me when I have reached my goal!

A New Start published by National Center for Youth Issues, Chattanooga, TN.

IMPORTANT FACTS TO REMEMBER

- Set realistic and measurable goals for yourself.

- Your realistic goals can be achieved if you believe that they can truly happen.

- It will help you to achieve your goals if you keep the end result (the picture of the whole new you!) in your mind at all times.

- Nobody is perfect. If you experience a set-back, just try again!

- Don't eat in front of the TV. You might end up eating more than you ever planned.

- Eat small bites slowly. You will realize when you are full!

- Think for yourself. Don't be ruled by what your friends are eating or what a TV commercial suggests you should eat.

- Move around as much as possible. Remember that the USDA says that kids should get an hour of exercise a day.

- Drink water instead of sugary soda and juices.

- Drink low-fat milk. (Children under two can ignore this advice!)

- Plan your meals using the USDA Food Pyramid.

- Plan the amounts you will eat using the USDA dietary guidelines.

- Make sugary or salty "junk food" an occasional treat, not an everyday occurrence.

- Eat healthy snacks, such as plain popcorn, raw vegetables, fruit and nuts.

- Don't skip meals or try to go on a diet. That doesn't work!

- Don't eat snacks before bedtime.

- Don't eat to reward yourself for a good day or console yourself for a bad day. Find other ways to feel good about yourself.

A New Start published by National Center for Youth Issues, Chattanooga, TN.

EFFECTIVE GOAL SETTING

The same goal-setting guidelines are true for any type of goal you want to achieve—whether you are setting goals for academic achievement, trying to improve your athletic abilities, or setting goals for weight and health improvement.

*Any goal you set must be both **REALISTIC** and **MEASURABLE!***

REALISTIC

⊙ *You must realize that goals are NOT wishes. The goals you make have to be possible.*

Never say, *"My goal is to lose 50 pounds before next weekend,"* This is an unrealistic goal. You will be disappointed because it is not going to happen. It is impossible.

⊙ *The goal has to be realistic and in your control.*

"My goal is to win the lottery," This is a wish over which you have no control. While it might possibly happen, it would be because of luck, not something that you worked to achieve.

MEASURABLE

⊙ *When you set a goal, you must be able to tell whether or not you reached it. You have to be specific about what you are working toward.*

If you say, *"My goal is to eat better,"* You are not being clear about what you are trying to accomplish. What does "better" mean? How would you know if you were doing it?

If you say, *"My goal is to be healthy,"* Again, this is not clear. What would healthy mean? How would you know if you were healthy?

The following are examples of goals that are *REALISTIC* and *MEASURABLE!*

I will not gain any weight this week.
   Could this happen?
      (Yes)
   Can you tell if it happened?
      (Yes, you could weigh
      yourself on a scale each day.)

57

Another thing to consider when writing goals is that there are long-term goals and short-term goals.

LONG-TERM AND SHORT-TERM GOALS

A long-term goal is something that you are working to achieve in the future.

- ● *"I will go to college and study to be a teacher."*

    Is that realistic?

    (Yes)

    Is it measurable?

    (Yes, you would know if you accomplished it.)

This goal will not be proven until years from today. You might be currently in 4th grade, so achieving this goal will not happen for quite a few years. It is a good thing to make long-term goals, but to accomplish them, you have to break them down and start with some short-term goals that you could begin now.

The following are short term goals that might help you achieve your long-term goal to go to college and become a teacher.

- ● *"I will do all of my work this week in school."*
- ● *"I will study at least an hour for every test I will have this week."*
- ● *"I will begin a savings account and save $5.00 every week."*

Each one of these short-term goals is realistic (they could happen) and measurable (you will know if you accomplish it).

When it comes to weight management, there are long-term and short-term goals. In the story,

Randall did not want to sit at the back table. A long-term goal he might have set would be to be able to sit in a student-sized desk. That goal would take some time to accomplish, so to make it happen, he set short-term goals.

- ● *"I will follow the guidelines recommended by the USDA Food Pyramid."*
- ● *"I will eat only one junk food item each week."*
- ● *"I will get 60 minutes of exercise each day."*

These are all realistic and measurable short-term goals that would help him reach his long-term goal of fitting in a student-sized desk.

Write your realistic and measurable long-term goals on the lines below:

_____

_____

_____

_____

_____

_____

_____

What short-term goals will you need to set to make the long-term goals above come true?

_____

_____

_____

_____

_____

_____

"A New Start" Contract

To be completed by child:

I want to be healthy and fit. In order to do this I will honor the following contract:

I, _____ ,
(child's name)
promise to do my best to make major changes in my lifestyle.

On the following pages, I will set goals to eat the right amount of healthy foods. I will do my best to get one hour of exercise a day.

On the following pages, I will set detailed eating and exercise goals.

I know these new changes will be difficult, but I will make a picture of the healthy me in my head and I will keep this picture fresh in my mind at all times. I am committed to make "A New Start" work for me!

_____
Child's Signature

_____
Date

To be completed by parent:

I want to help my child with "A New Start."

I, _____ ,
(parent's name)
promise to do my best to be a good role model when it comes to healthy eating and proper exercise.

I will purchase vegetables, fruits, low-fat dairy items, lean meats, poultry and whole grain products for my family. I will limit the amount of junk food that will be available to my child.

I will encourage my child to get an hour of exercise a day. Our family will do activities together to promote health and energy for all.

_____
Parent's Signature

_____
Date

A New Start published by National Center for Youth Issues, Chattanooga, TN.

FOOd Guide Pyramid

FOR YOUng Children

A Daily Guide for 2- to 6-Year-Olds

60

Fats & Sweets — Eat LESS

MILK Group — 2 servings

MEAT Group — 2 servings

VEGETABLE Group — 3 servings

FRUIT Group — 2 servings

GRAIN Group 6 servings

US Department of Agriculture;
Center For Nutrition Policy and Promotion

USDA is an equal opportunity provider and employer.

A New Start published by National Center for Youth Issues, Chattanooga, TN.

FOOD GUIDE PYRAMID
FOR CHILDREN OVER 6 & ADULTS

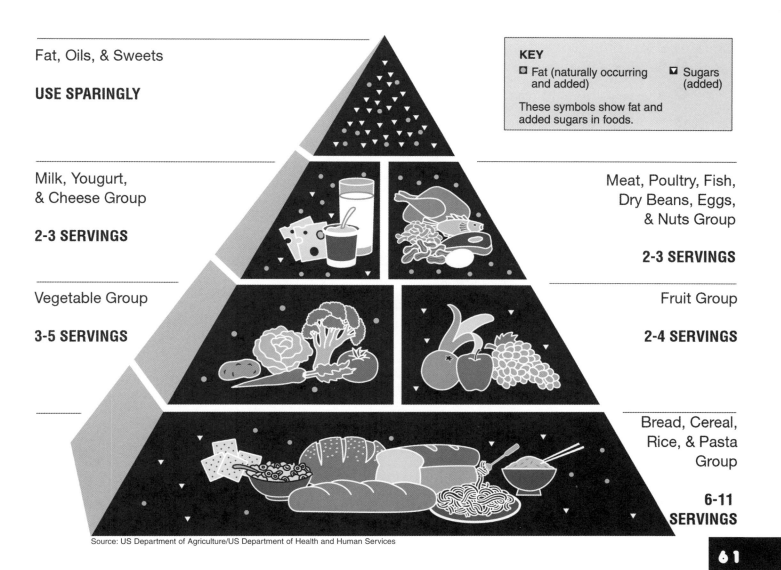

Fat, Oils, & Sweets

USE SPARINGLY

KEY
□ Fat (naturally occurring and added)　　☑ Sugars (added)

These symbols show fat and added sugars in foods.

Milk, Yougurt, & Cheese Group

2-3 SERVINGS

Meat, Poultry, Fish, Dry Beans, Eggs, & Nuts Group

2-3 SERVINGS

Vegetable Group

3-5 SERVINGS

Fruit Group

2-4 SERVINGS

Bread, Cereal, Rice, & Pasta Group

6-11 SERVINGS

Source: US Department of Agriculture/US Department of Health and Human Services

61

EATING GUIDELINES FROM THE USDA

The Food Pyramid suggests that a child 2-6 years old eat the following each day:

- 6 servings from the grain group
- 3 servings from the vegetable group
- 2 servings from the fruit group
- 2 servings from the milk, cheese and yogurt group
- 2 servings from the meat, poultry, fish, dry beans, eggs and nuts group

For children over the age of 6, the numbers vary a little:

- 6-11 servings from the grain group
- 3-5 servings from the vegetable group
- 2-4 servings from the fruit group
- 2-3 servings from the milk, cheese and yogurt group
- 2-3 servings from the meat, poultry, fish, dry beans, eggs and nuts group

WHAT COUNTS AS A SERVING?

Grain Group

- 1 slice of bread
- About 1 cup of cereal
- 1 cup of cooked cereal, rice or pasta
- 1 bagel

Vegetable Group

- 1 cup of raw leafy vegetables
- 1 cup of other vegetables, cooked or raw
- 1 cup of vegetable juice

Fruit Group

- 1 medium apple, banana, orange or pear
- 1 cup of chopped, cooked or canned pears
- 1 cup of fruit juice

Milk, Yogurt, and Cheese Group

- 1 cup of milk or yogurt
- 1 ounce of natural cheese (such as Cheddar)
- 2 ounces of processed cheese (such as American)

Meat, Poultry, Fish, Dry Beans, Eggs, and Nuts Group

- 2-3 ounces of cooked lean meat, poultry or fish
- 1 cup of cooked dry beans
- 2 Tablespoons of peanut butter counts as-1 ounce of lean meat
- 1 egg counts as-1 ounce of lean meat

A New Start published by National Center for Youth Issues, Chattanooga, TN.

ADDITIONAL GUIDELINES FROM THE USDA

Grain Group

Choose whole grains when possible. Whole grains are healthier because they have more vitamins, minerals, and fiber than refined white versions. The high fiber content may help you to feel full with fewer calories. Brown rice, oatmeal and whole wheat are good choices in the grain group.

Vegetable & Fruit Group

Be sure to eat a variety of colors of fruits and vegetables. Dark green leafy vegetables and deeply colored fruits are especially rich in many nutrients. Most fruits and vegetables are naturally low in fat and calories and are filling. Eating the whole fruit or vegetable is healthier than drinking the juice of the same items. Choose fruit for desserts instead of sugary items.

Milk, Yogurt, and Cheese Group

For good heart health choose low-fat versions of these dairy products. They will be healthier and lower in calories for a growing child. Children under the age of two should not follow this rule and need the fat from whole milk products.

Meat, Poultry, Fish, Dry Beans, Eggs, and Nuts Group

Choose lean meat with the fat trimmed away. Take the skin off of poultry. Limit your intake of high-fat processed meat like bacon, salami, sausages, bologna and other cold cuts.

On the following lines, list some foods from each group that you will be sure to eat on your "New Start." Do some research at the grocery store and include some foods that you have never tasted before. Put a star by those items that you will be eating for the first time!

Grain Group

_____

_____

_____

_____

_____

Vegetable Group

_____

_____

_____

_____

Fruit Group

_____

_____

_____

_____

_____

Milk Group

_____

_____

_____

_____

Meat Group

_____

_____

_____

_____

_____

And don't forget to drink lots of WATER!

A New Start published by National Center for Youth Issues, Chattanooga, TN.

MY WEEKLY MENU

An eating plan for the week of: _____

This chart lists the food groups and the number of servings that you should eat each day. Make your plan for a week. Circle the corresponding number when you write a serving from that group. For example, if you plan orange juice and oatmeal at breakfast, write the words "juice" and "oatmeal" and circle 1 in the Fruit group and 1 in the Grain group. The servings in parentheses are optional.

Group	Sunday	Monday	Tuesday	Wednesday	Thursday	Friday	Saturday
Dairy	1 2 (3)	1 2 (3)	1 2 (3)	1 2 (3)	1 2 (3)	1 2 (3)	1 2 (3)
Meat, Poultry, etc.	1 2 (3)	1 2 (3)	1 2 (3)	1 2 (3)	1 2 (3)	1 2 (3)	1 2 (3)
Vegetable	1 2 3 (4) (5)	1 2 3 (4) (5)	1 2 3 (4) (5)	1 2 3 (4) (5)	1 2 3 (4) (5)	1 2 3 (4) (5)	1 2 3 (4) (5)
Fruit	1 2 (3) (4)	1 2 (3) (4)	1 2 (3) (4)	1 2 (3) (4)	1 2 (3) (4)	1 2 (3) (4)	1 2 (3) (4)
Bread & Grains	1 2 3 4 5 6 (7) (8) (9) (10) (11)	1 2 3 4 5 6 (7) (8) (9) (10) (11)	1 2 3 4 5 6 (7) (8) (9) (10) (11)	1 2 3 4 5 6 (7) (8) (9) (10) (11)	1 2 3 4 5 6 (7) (8) (9) (10) (11)	1 2 3 4 5 6 (7) (8) (9) (10) (11)	1 2 3 4 5 6 (7) (8) (9) (10) (11)

Breakfast

Snack

Lunch

Snack

Dinner

A New Start published by National Center for Youth Issues, Chattanooga, TN.

MY FOOD JOURNAL

For the week of _____

Many people eat more than they think they do! It is easy to eat mindlessly and without realizing the quantity of food you have consumed—especially in front of the television set!

Make copies of this page and use it as a journal to keep a list of what you eat each day. Be sure to write down every single bite of food that you eat!

Sunday
Breakfast _____
Lunch _____
Dinner _____
Snacks _____

Monday
Breakfast _____
Lunch _____
Dinner _____
Snacks _____

Tuesday
Breakfast _____
Lunch _____
Dinner _____
Snacks _____

Wednesday
Breakfast _____
Lunch _____
Dinner _____
Snacks _____

Thursday
Breakfast _____
Lunch _____
Dinner _____
Snacks _____

Friday
Breakfast _____
Lunch _____
Dinner _____
Snacks _____

Saturday
Breakfast _____
Lunch _____
Dinner _____
Snacks _____

A New Start published by National Center for Youth Issues, Chattanooga, TN.

THE BENEFITS OF EXERCISE

There are many reasons why exercise is good for you. The USDA and DHHS suggest that adults should exercise for at least 30 minutes a day and children should exercise for 60 minutes a day. This doesn't mean that you have to do jumping jacks or sit-ups for the whole hour. Have fun, run around, play soccer, dance or jump rope. The time will go by before you know it. Also, helping your mom do housework is great exercise. (You will be doing your required exercise and you will be making your mom very happy too!)

Remember to consider all the safety factors when you exercise. Always wear appropriate shoes and perform the exercise on an appropriate surface. If the situation calls for it, wear reflective tape or lights and a helmet, and carry identification. Exercise with a group so you will stay safe. You'll also have more fun! Don't forget to drink water before, during, and after exercise.

Below are just a few of the benefits you will gain from doing exercise!

- Builds self-esteem
- Controls appetite
- Reduces stress
- Gives you more energy
- Builds muscles
- Increases flexibility

- Strengthens bone
- Reduces fat
- Maintains strength
- Helps your posture
- It's fun!

MY EXERCISE GOALS

For the week of _____

- The USDA and the DHHS recommend that healthy children get 60 minutes of exercise a day.

- It is always a good idea to be checked by a doctor before starting a new exercise program.

- Once you have your doctor's okay, start making goals and planning different ways you will get your 60 minutes of exercise each day. Have fun, run, jump, dance, or help your mom by vaccuuming. Be creative! Try to move as many muscles as you can.

- Think about the ways you will exercise and fill out the following chart each week.

My goal is to get_____minutes of exercise every day. This is what I will do each day.

Sunday

Exercise Type	Minutes
Exercise Type	Minutes
Exercise Type	Minutes

Monday

Exercise Type	Minutes
Exercise Type	Minutes
Exercise Type	Minutes

Tuesday

Exercise Type	Minutes
Exercise Type	Minutes
Exercise Type	Minutes

Wednesday

Exercise Type	Minutes
Exercise Type	Minutes
Exercise Type	Minutes

Thursday

Exercise Type	Minutes
Exercise Type	Minutes
Exercise Type	Minutes

Friday

Exercise Type	Minutes
Exercise Type	Minutes
Exercise Type	Minutes

Saturday

Exercise Type	Minutes
Exercise Type	Minutes
Exercise Type	Minutes

A New Start published by National Center for Youth Issues, Chattanooga, TN.

MY EXERCISE JOURNAL

For the week of _____

Are you getting your daily 60 minutes of exercise in each day? Keep a record of what you have done. If you exercise vigorously, you are exercising your muscles, your heart and your lungs, and you are burning lots of calories.

Make copies of this worksheet, so that you can continue to keep track of your exercise schedule. Be sure to write down what you did for exercise each day. Also write how many minutes you did it.

Sunday

Exercise: _____ Minutes: _____

Exercise: _____ Minutes: _____

Exercise: _____ Minutes: _____

Monday

Exercise: _____ Minutes: _____

Exercise: _____ Minutes: _____

Exercise: _____ Minutes: _____

Tuesday

Exercise: _____ Minutes: _____

Exercise: _____ Minutes: _____

Exercise: _____ Minutes: _____

Wednesday

Exercise: _____ Minutes: _____

Exercise: _____ Minutes: _____

Exercise: _____ Minutes: _____

Thursday

Exercise: _____ Minutes: _____

Exercise: _____ Minutes: _____

Exercise: _____ Minutes: _____

Friday

Exercise: _____ Minutes: _____

Exercise: _____ Minutes: _____

Exercise: _____ Minutes: _____

Saturday

Exercise: _____ Minutes: _____

Exercise: _____ Minutes: _____

Exercise: _____ Minutes: _____

68

JUMPING ROPE CAN BE FUN!

As you begin "A New Start" you will want to add lots of exercise to your routine. The USDA suggests that children get one hour of exercise every day. When starting a new program like this, it is always good to get an okay from your doctor, especially if you have been very inactive in the past. Once the doctor approves, try a new "old way" of getting exercise. Try jumping rope!

Kids have jumped rope for hundreds of years. It is a great exercise that strengthens muscles and bones and it is a good workout for your heart and lungs, which helps get oxygen to your brain.

The best thing about jumping rope is that it is very cheap and easy to do. You don't have to buy or rent expensive equipment, or wait until you have a team to do it. Just find a rope, go out on the porch and jump!

The right size jump rope can make the exercise easier. Stand in the middle of the rope and pull up the ends. The ends should come up to your armpits.

To turn the rope, you should not swing your arms all the way around. Keep your elbows close to or beside your body, put your hands out to your sides and turn the rope with your wrists.

When you jump, be sure to land lightly on the balls of your feet. You don't have to jump high, just enough to clear the rope. You can jump and then take a little bounce between each jump or jump continually without the bounce.

Once you learn the basics, you can add tricks. Create your own tricks by turning the rope at different speeds, or try jumping with a partner, or try jumping in and out of a rope as it is being turned by another person.

If you don't think you can make up your own tricks, ask your parents if you can use a computer and go on the Internet. Using any search engine, type in "Jump Rope Tricks" and you will find many tricks described in detail. There are even pictures of real kids in real jump rope clubs all over the United States.

Try jumping rope. You'll be healthy, you'll burn calories and you'll have fun!

A New Start published by National Center for Youth Issues, Chattanooga, TN.

JUMP ROPE RHYMES

Jumping rope to rhymes can make this activity more fun and challenging. Try saying the following verses as you jump rope. Set goals to extend your jumping time and continue to set new records.

If you are interested in finding more rhymes, ask your parents if you can use a computer and go on the Internet. Using any search engine, type in "Jump Rope Rhymes" and you will be amazed to find hundreds of rhymes that have been used for years.

1 Count toward Health!

I want to be healthy,

I want to be fit.

I'll jump this rope

And not just sit!

Jumping rope is so much fun

I feel great when I get done

How many jumps can I do,

I'll let you know when I get through!

One, Two, Three … (count until you miss)

2 Good Foods

Cauliflower, broccoli, carrots and peas,

Blueberries, apples and cottage cheese.

Healthy foods will make me strong,

And this will last my whole life long!

3 New Start

I'm gonna' change my life and get a new start,

Jumping rope is good for my heart.

If I eat good foods and move around,

Toward health and fitness I'll be bound!

A New Start published by National Center for Youth Issues, Chattanooga, TN.

"A New Start" Rap

This can be said as a jump rope rhyme
or simply as a rap. Memorize it and say
it when you need a little motivation!

I'm gonna' change my life.
And make a "new start."

I can do what I dream,
I'm brave and I'm smart.

I'll set some goals,
And make 'em come true.

I won't give up,
I'll try until I do!

This is my time,
I want it to be right.

I deserve what's best,
My future looks bright!

I am going to make this change,
I want it from my heart.

So today is the day
For my brand "new start!"

A New Start published by National Center for Youth Issues, Chattanooga, TN.

A NOTE TO PARENTS

Childhood obesity is a seriously growing problem. One out of five children are overweight in the United States and 10% of all children are obese. These statistics are frightening, even more so because they have doubled over the past 15 years.

Childhood obesity is a topic that we have heard a lot about recently on the news, in magazines, and on TV, because it poses such a major threat to our children. Besides being linked to physical problems such as heart disease, stroke and diabetes, we all know that obese children often suffer from social and emotional problems that often follow them into adulthood.

Obesity is now considered to be a leading cause of death in our country. The saddest part about all of it is … that it is PREVENTABLE!

How can we prevent obesity in our children?

The first thing parents must realize is that children learn more from them than from any other source. Kids look to their role models for guidance.

So we, as parents, must guide our children to healthy eating and good exercise habits. If a parent doesn't serve vegetables, the children will certainly not learn to like vegetables. If a parent flops down in front of the TV and gets little or no physical exercise, the children will learn that type of behavior.

In our country, many people eat too much of the wrong foods. Our serving sizes have grown to a point that we don't even realize how much the proper amount is. We are a society that is in a hurry and many of us eat a lot of fast foods that don't always offer the proper nutrients.

To prevent obesity in children, we need to relearn how to eat and exercise properly! We, as adults, have to learn to control our own behaviors to save our children.

Should we teach our children to diet?

No. That is not the way to good health! Tackling the problem of obesity in children is difficult because there is a fine line between beginning a program of healthy eating and going on a DIET. We have to be careful because we don't want to raise children who feel guilty about their eating habits or develop eating disorders. The dieting lifestyle has led many adults to yo-yo dieting, fad diets, binge eating, and misery, and we must try to save our children from that kind of life.

So how do we teach our children the right way to think about food?

Again, it is the parents who must model healthy habits that are consistent and steady. For the sake of our children, we must all get regular exercise and eat a variety of fruits, vegetables, whole grain products, lean meats and poultry and low-fat dairy items. We have to show kids that it is not okay to skip meals or starve and then binge. Remember, that every behavior we exhibit, is being closely watched and repeated in the next generation at an earlier age than ever before. If your family has had poor eating and exercise habits in the past, let your children know that this "new start" program is a permanent change. Then do your best to stick to that promise.

We should show our children that sugary and high-fat junk foods are just occasional treats. We should talk to children about the commercials that tempt us to buy things that aren't always good for us.

Family time can be a time of energetic activity rather than watching TV. We can tell children that the rule is to not eat in front of the TV. We can teach them that portions are often the problem, not what is being eaten. And we can offer lots of healthy foods and show them that we are always open to trying new foods. Without forcing them to eat healthy foods, we can keep offering it to them. If they don't eat it, we shouldn't follow up with an alternate junk food choice.

We shouldn't force our children to eat every bite on their plates. Young children are often better at judging how much is enough than their parents are. We can teach them that a variety of fruit, vegetables, lean meats and low-fat dairy items are a way of life.

In the story, "A New Start," Randall's mom told him that he was just big for his age and that he had baby fat. She fed him his favorite "comfort foods" and kept the cookie jar well-stocked. She didn't set out to make him fat. She did everything out of love, but thankfully came to realize that this kind of love wasn't helping him to have a quality life.

We need to stop feeding kids the wrong things out of love, as a reward, and as a "special treat." Ignoring a child's problem with weight is not going to make it disappear.

The problem of obesity can be conquered, but it will take everyone working together. The way to help children is by making changes in our own eating and exercise habits.

While it is a very difficult task, it can be done. Do it for the children! Your whole family can enjoy a healthy "NEW START!"

73

GLOSSARY

calories – Calories are measurements of energy which are used as fuel by the human body. Human beings need fuel for energy the same way a car needs gasoline. Food contains calories-the amount of energy the food item contains. If a person doesn't move and get enough exercise, the calories he or she gets from eating food are not all burned and the liver changes the surplus calories into fat that is stored for future energy needs. If the person consistently doesn't exercise, the deposited fat storage keeps building and the person could become overweight or obese.

comfort foods – This term is used to describe food that gives comfort or reminds a person of home and love. Unfortunately, most of the time, comfort foods are high in sugar and high in fat. Cookies, pastries, fried foods, chips and ice cream are examples of the types of foods considered to be "comfort foods."

empty calories – All food contains calories. Foods that are good for us also contain a lot of vitamins and minerals, which our bodies need to stay healthy. However, some junk foods have a lot of calories but no nutritional value. Therefore, the calories provided in this type of food are called "empty calories."

emotional eating – Some people eat when they are sad or happy … for consolation or a reward. Food is fuel to be used for energy and should not be used for emotional reasons. When food is used as an emotional crutch, the results might produce weight problems. This then becomes a negative cycle, since the person might feel bad about his or her weight and then eat more for emotional consolation.

energy – Energy is the power needed for human existence. Human beings need energy to breathe, move and pump blood. They acquire this energy from food. If we take in more calories than our body can use, the surplus will turn into fat.

junk food – Foods that have empty calories are known as junk food. These foods are often high in fat and sugar and have little nutritional value.

obesity – A person who has an excessive amount of fat stored in his or her body is known to be suffering from obesity. The adjective to describe the person is "obese." Most definitions say that an obese person is 20 – 30% over their ideal weight. Obesity is a growing problem in our country and the problems associated with obesity are a leading cause of death in the United States.

sugar – The USDA has stated that the average American eats over 150 pounds of sugar a year. Sugary foods often contain a high calorie level, so this consumption of sugar can be related to the problem of obesity. The USDA recommends that we limit our sugar consumption to 10 teaspoons a day. A can of soda contains about the equivalent of 15 teaspoons of sugar so drinking a soda each day has already put us over the limit! An additional problem we might have if we are trying to limit our sugar intake is that there are hidden sugars in many foods. Reading a label will help you be aware of all the sugar you are eating. For example, sugar is an ingredient in peanut butter, mayonnaise, and spaghetti sauce. Be sure to look for other names of sugar such as dextrose, fructose, corn syrup, and high fructose corn syrup when reading the labels on food products.

QUESTIONS

A New Start published by National Center for Youth Issues, Chattanooga, TN.

QUESTIONS

Questions about "A New Start"

1. Name at least four things that Randall and his mother were doing at the beginning of the story that contributed to their obesity.

_____

_____

_____

_____

2. Why did Randall and his mom want to begin "A New Start" with a contract?

_____

_____

_____

_____

3. What were some of the comfort foods that Randall loved? What are some of your favorite comfort foods? What is wrong with using food as comfort?

_____

_____

_____

_____

4. Randall tried to ignore the mean comments about his weight. Describe a time when you have had another child say something mean about you. What did you do about it?

_____

_____

_____

_____

5. Name at least four things Randall did after beginning his "New Start" to improve and change his lifestyle.

_____

_____

_____

_____

6. In the end of the story, on the first day of 5th grade, Randall's mother packed his lunch for him. Why do you think she did this?

_____

_____

_____

_____

7. Why is it important to eat using the USDA Food Pyramid as a guide?

_____

_____

_____

_____

8. What problems could result from eating many of your meals at a restaurant or fast food store?

_____

_____

_____

_____

9. How could reading the labels on packages of food help you eat the proper amount? What else can you learn from reading the labels?

_____

_____

_____

_____

10. Why did Randall and his mom want to use the USDA and DHHS agencies as their resource on how to fight obesity?

_____

_____

_____

_____

11. If one of your friends is overweight or obese, what can you do to help?

_____

_____

_____

_____

12. Why do you think the problem of obesity is growing in our country?

_____

_____

_____

_____

13. If a child has a weight problem, what can he or she do to solve the problem? Who should be part of the plan?

_____

_____

_____

_____

14. Before starting a new program of diet and exercise, with whom should a person consult? Why?

_____

_____

_____

_____

15. List at least two reasons why beginning a program of healthy eating and exercise would be beneficial.

_____

_____

_____

_____

77

Questions about being Overweight

78

1. In the story, Randall's mother had been overweight as a child. How might parents' practices and attitudes be passed on to their children?

_____

_____

_____

_____

2. Do you think there could be other reasons people might be overweight even though they don't eat a lot?

_____

_____

_____

_____

3. Randall found out that overweight people sometimes have health problems. What are some problems related to being overweight?

_____

_____

_____

_____

4. Besides being physically uncomfortable, what other problems might an overweight child have?

_____

_____

_____

_____

5. If you know someone who is overweight, what could you do to help that person?

_____

_____

_____

_____

6. Randall's mother loved him very much. Why did she feed him a lot of junk food?

_____

_____

_____

_____

7. What problems could an overweight child have when going clothes shopping?

_____

_____

_____

_____

Questions about Food

1. Name the food groups listed on the USDA Food Pyramid.

_____

_____

_____

_____

2. How could you help your parents plan for a grocery shopping trip?

_____

_____

_____

_____

3. The following are sections at a grocery store. Name four nutritious items from each section.

   Dairy

   _____

   _____

   _____

   _____

   Fruits

   _____

   _____

   _____

   _____

Vegetables

_____

_____

_____

_____

Meats

_____

_____

_____

_____

Canned Foods

_____

_____

_____

_____

4. In the story, Randall decided that it wasn't a good idea to eat while watching TV. Why? Where should you eat your meals?

_____

_____

_____

_____

79

Questions about Exercise

1. List at least three types of exercise
    that could be played with two teams.

    _____

    _____

    _____

    _____

2. List at least three types of exercise
    that you could do by yourself.

    _____

    _____

    _____

    _____

3. What would be a good exercise
    that your family could do together?

    _____

    _____

    _____

    _____

4. What is a type of exercise that you
    and your friends could do at school?

    _____

    _____

    _____

    _____

5. What are some things your school
    does to encourage students to move
    around and get exercise?

    _____

    _____

    _____

    _____

6. Research says that kids who watch a
    lot of TV or play too many hours of video
    games have a tendency to be overweight.
    Why do you think this is true?

    _____

    _____

    _____

7. What do you think is the
    most fun kind of exercise?

    _____

    _____

    _____

    _____

MAKING WISE CHOICES

Circle the one food in each group below that
might not be a healthy choice on a daily basis.
(It's okay to have a treat every once in a while.)
Remember to think before you pop something
in your mouth!

1. water
   orange juice
   soda
   low-fat milk

2. turkey
   chicken
   fish
   fudge

3. corn
   corn curls
   string beans
   broccoli

4. donuts
   whole wheat bread
   unsweetened cereals
   brown rice

5. bananas
   apples
   oranges
   fruit punch

6. potatoes
   french fries
   sweet potatoes
   beans

7. grilled beef
   tuna
   fried steak
   broiled pork chops

8. lemons
   grapes
   fruit-flavored candy
   blueberries

9. potato chips
   cauliflower
   asparagus
   spinach

10. lettuce
   tomatoes
   radishes
   red licorice

81

A New Start published by National Center for Youth Issues, Chattanooga, TN.

ANSWER KEY

Answers to Questions about "A New Start"

1. Practices that contributed to the obesity of Randall and his mother were: eating foods that were high in fat and sugar on a daily basis, eating in front of the TV, not getting enough exercise, eating portions that were too large, and eating for emotional reasons.

2. Randall and his mom both wanted to be certain about what their goal was and what they needed to do to reach this goal. They wanted it to be "in writing" so that they could officially begin "A New Start" and stick to it conscientiously.

3. Randall loved cookies, chips and junk foods. It is wrong to use food to console yourself when you are unhappy because it is like you are using food like a drug! Food is supposed to be eaten because a person is hungry and needs nourishment, not because the person is sad or mad.

4. Any answer.

5. Some of the habits Randall improved upon were: he watched how much he ate, he used the USDA Food Pyramid as a guide, he got an hour of exercise a day, he stopped drinking sodas and sugary juices, he drank lots of water, he stopped eating in front of the TV and he ate healthy snacks instead of the cookies he used as comfort.

6. Randall and his mom are trying to carefully follow the guidelines from the USDA guidelines. His mom packed him a healthy lunch that was well balanced and nutritious. School lunches might include some unhealthy choices and Randall wanted to make the choices at home when he could take some time to think about it.

7. Many people have gotten in the habit of eating too much or eating too much of the wrong type of foods. We often watch TV commercials and choose the wrong foods or overeat at a restaurant. Using the USDA Food Pyramid as a guide helps a person to plan a well-balanced meal and eat the right amount.

8. Restaurants serve big portions of food. In fact, many restaurants brag about having the largest portions or an "all you can eat" policy. If you eat in restaurants, you have to be very careful to eat the proper amount. Fast food stores sell many foods that have empty calories. In other words, the foods are full of calories, with little nutrition.

9. You can learn a lot from reading a label. You can find out about the ingredients, which are listed in order from most to least. If a spaghetti sauce lists tomatoes, sugar, spices, etc., you know you are eating some hidden sugar, because it is the second item on the list. The label also tells how much a serving size is. Some packages of food that seem small might be meant for two or three servings.

A New Start published by National Center for Youth Issues, Chattanooga, TN.

10. Randall's mom suggested using information from the government agencies because this information has been well researched and comes from a reputable source. There is a lot of information from various sources about fad diets and suggestions for weight loss that might not be healthy for a child.

11. The best thing you could do for an overweight friend is just be his or her friend. If you call attention to the extra weight or suggest a diet, you might hurt your friend's feelings. It is up to your friend and his or her family to find out about weight loss.

    Another thing you can do is be a good role model for healthy eating and exercise. Suggest playing games that involve movement when your friend asks you to play.

12. The problem of obesity is growing. Kids are eating a lot of the wrong foods because it is all around us. Every time you turn on the TV, you see lots of tempting food commercials. Also, kids are not exercising as much as they did in the past. This could be because the TV is readily available and we now have more computers and computer games. Also, it is not always safe for a child to go out and play with friends without adult supervision. Kids might use that as an excuse for not getting the exercise they need.

13. If a child has a weight problem, he or she needs to talk to his parents about wanting to change eating and exercise habits. Then together, the child and the parents can create a sensible eating and exercise plan.

14. When someone is overweight, a doctor should check that person, if possible, before starting a new plan. The child might have some hidden health problems that could make strenuous exercise dangerous. As mentioned in the story, a child should not go on a diet to lose weight. The goal should be not to gain weight while growing into their current weight. A doctor can help by giving suggestions and approving the plan.

15. One reason that beginning a program of healthy eating and exercise would be beneficial is that the person will feel better physically. The person will have more energy and strength for life's challenges. The second reason is that the person might feel better about himself or herself. Overweight children are often teased and belittled, which can make self-esteem suffer. Feeling that you are the best that you can be helps a person feel successful!

A New Start published by National Center for Youth Issues, Chattanooga, TN.

Answers to Questions about being Overweight

1. Parents' practices and attitudes are formed when they are young. If they learn to overeat and get little exercise as children, then that is what they will teach their children. Unfortunately it is a cycle that continues unless something is done to break it.

2. Some people don't eat very much and are still overweight. Some medicines that people take cause weight gain. Sometimes the person's body uses calories more slowly and they must exercise more than other people to get their metabolism going.

3. Some health problems that overweight people have are heart problems, diabetes and blood pressure problems. Any organ of the body might be challenged if excess fat is covering it. This could lead to a number of difficulties.

4. Overweight children are often teased and belittled by other children. It is hard to have good self-esteem when treated in this way.

5. To help an overweight person, be a friend. Like them for who they are, and don't call attention to the weight problem. Be a good role model by eating healthy foods and getting a lot of exercise. Encourage them to join you in your activities.

6. Randall's mother loved him and gave him treats and special rewards because of this love. She knew how much he enjoyed eating sweets and let him have these things because she loved him. She also didn't realize that his weight was becoming such a problem for him.

7. Stylish clothes are often made in small sizes. Some children have to buy adult-sized clothes to get them to fit. The adult sizes are not designed for children's taste in clothes.

Answers to Questions about Food

1. The food groups are: Bread, Cereal, Rice and Pasta Group; Fruit and Vegetable Group; Meat, Poultry, Fish, Beans, Eggs and Nuts Group; Milk, Yogurt and Cheese Group; and Fats, Oils and Sweets Group.

2. You could help your parents plan a grocery trip by studying the food groups and picking out food from each group. It would be a good idea to sit down with your parents and help plan the meals for the week.

3. *Dairy:* low-fat milk, low-fat cheese, yogurt, etc.

   Fruits: bananas, apples, berries, pineapple, etc.

   Vegetables: string beans, spinach, carrots, broccoli, lettuce, etc.

   Meats: lean beef, fish, chicken, turkey, pork, etc.

   Canned foods: canned tomatoes, beans, various vegetables, etc.

4. If you eat while you watch TV, you aren't paying attention to how much you eat. You often eat more than you realize. Also, watching commercials about fast foods might make you feel hungry. It is better to eat your meals sitting down at the kitchen or dining room table.

Answers to Questions about Exercise

1. Types of exercise that could be played with two teams are baseball, kickball, soccer, touch football, etc.

2. Types of exercise that you could do by yourself are jumping rope, walking, running, shooting baskets, riding a bike, etc.

3. A family walk would be a nice activity. Of course, families have all kinds of different interests. Therefore a family might want to play golf, frisbee, softball, ride bikes, etc.

4. Childhood games, such as tag, playing catch and kickball are fun and good exercise.

5. Most schools try to get children to be active in Physical Education class (gym class) or at recess. Some special events are planned to include physical activities.

6. If you sit and eat, you are not burning any calories, just taking them in. People also often eat more than they realize in front of the TV.

7. Answers will vary.

85

Answers to Making Wise Choices

1. soda

2. fudge

3. corn curls

4. donuts

5. fruit punch

6. french fries

7. fried steak

8. fruit flavored candy

9. potato chips

10. red licorice

A New Start published by National Center for Youth Issues, Chattanooga, TN.

RES**O**URCES

U. S. Department of Agriculture (USDA)

U. S. Department of Health and Human Services (DHHS)

Web sites for Dietary Guidelines for Americans (updated in 2000):

http://health.gov/dietaryguidelines

Food Pyramid graphics:

http://www.usda.gov/cnpp/pyramid.html

Some additional web sites for kids:

USA Jump Rope – http://www.usajrf.org

Food quizzes and games – http://www.nal.usda.gov/fnic/etext/000100.html

Why Exercise is Cool – http://kidshealth.org/kid/stay_healthy/fit/work_it_out.html

Some additional web sites for parents: (Related articles)

http://www.kinderstart.com/foodandnutrition

http://www.nal.usda.gov.fnic/etext/000060.html

http://www.healthierus.gov/exercise.html

A New Start published by National Center for Youth Issues, Chattanooga, TN.